SO-ARS-555

Put Beginning Readers on the Right Track with
ALL ABOARD READING™

The All Aboard Reading series is especially designed for beginning readers. Written by noted authors and illustrated in full color, these are books that children really want to read—books to excite their imagination, expand their interests, make them laugh, and support their feelings. With fiction and nonfiction stories that are high interest and curriculum-related, All Aboard Reading books offer something for every young reader. And with four different reading levels, the All Aboard Reading series lets you choose which books are most appropriate for your children and their growing abilities.

Picture Readers
Picture Readers have super-simple texts, with many nouns appearing as rebus pictures. At the end of each book are 24 flash cards—on one side is a rebus picture; on the other side is the written-out word.

Station Stop 1
Station Stop 1 books are best for children who have just begun to read. Simple words and big type make these early reading experiences more comfortable. Picture clues help children to figure out the words on the page. Lots of repetition throughout the text helps children to predict the next word or phrase—an essential step in developing word recognition.

Station Stop 2
Station Stop 2 books are written specifically for children who are reading with help. Short sentences make it easier for early readers to understand what they are reading. Simple plots and simple dialogue help children with reading comprehension.

Station Stop 3
Station Stop 3 books are perfect for children who are reading alone. With longer text and harder words, these books appeal to children who have mastered basic reading skills. More complex stories captivate children who are ready for more challenging books.

In addition to All Aboard Reading books, look for All Aboard Math Readers™ (fiction stories that teach math concepts children are learning in school) and All Aboard Science Readers™ (nonfiction books that explore the most fascinating science topics in age-appropriate language).

All Aboard for happy reading!

To Jan—P.M.

Special thanks to Dr. Douglas Yanega of Riverside, CA.

Library of Congress Cataloging-in-Publication Data

Milton, Joyce.
  Honeybees / by Joyce Milton; illustrated by Pete Mueller.
    p. cm.–(All aboard science reader. Station stop 2)
Summary: Describes the anatomy, behavior, and life cycle of the honeybee, as well as the different kinds of honey that are produced on bee farms.
  1. Honeybee–Juvenile literature. [1. Honeybee. 2. Bees. 3. Honey.]
I. Mueller, Pete, ill. II. Title. III. Series: All aboard science reader. Station stop 2.
QL568.A6 M565 2003
595.79'9–dc21

                                          2002151247

ISBN 0-448-43142-4 (GB)   A B C D E F G H I J
ISBN 0-448-42846-6 (pb)   A B C D E F G H I J

Honeybees

By Joyce Milton
Illustrated by Pete Mueller

Grosset & Dunlap • New York

Where you see flowers,
you will often see bees.

In late spring,
gardens are filled
with honeybees.

There are many other kinds
of bees besides honeybees.

Sweat bee

Leaf-cutting bee

Plasterer bee

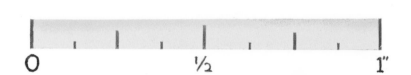
Bumblebee

0   ½   1"

Carpenter bee

Mining bee

Mason bee

Bees are insects, like flies
and ants and butterflies.
And like all insects,
they have six legs.
They have a body
with three parts to it.

Most kinds of wild bees live alone.
Each female bee lays her eggs
in her own nest.

But honeybees live
in a large group.
The group is called a colony.
Wild honeybee colonies
will find a tree or hollow log
in the woods.
They make a nest there.
The nest is also called a hive.

These wild honeybees are
buzzing all around.
They crawl over tulips
and other bright flowers.
What are the bees doing?
They are looking for nectar.
Nectar is a sweet juice in flowers.
Bees make honey from nectar.

This bee is drinking nectar.
Her long tongue is like a straw.
In one day
the bee will drink
from thousands of flowers.

The bee flies back
to the hive.
Other bees gather around.
They beg for nectar.
They stick their tongues
right in her mouth.
She spits up nectar for them.

She also does a special dance.

The dance tells other bees

where to find flowers.

The bees fly off.

They come back with nectar, too.

The bees spit out the nectar
drop by drop.
The nectar starts to dry
on their tongues.
Other bees fan their wings
very, very fast—
almost 200 times a second!
This also helps dry the nectar.

Soon it will be thick and smooth.

It will be . . . honey!

The honey you buy
at the market
does not come from wild bees.
It comes from bee farms.

The bees live
in man-made hives.
Man-made hives are big boxes.
As many as 50,000 bees
can live in a single hive.

Not all honey tastes the same.
Different flowers make
different nectar.
And nectar gives honey its flavor.
Clover honey is the most
popular honey in America.

Maybe you have heard
someone say,
"I'm as busy as a bee."
Well, hives <u>are</u> very busy places.

In every hive,
there are thousands of workers,
about 100 drones,
and one queen bee.

Worker bees have many jobs.
Besides making honey,
they also make wax.
It comes out of their bodies.

The workers use the wax
to build the rooms,
or cells, of the hive.
Each tiny cell has six sides.
Some cells are for storing nectar.

Besides nectar,
the worker bees
bring something else
from the garden—pollen.

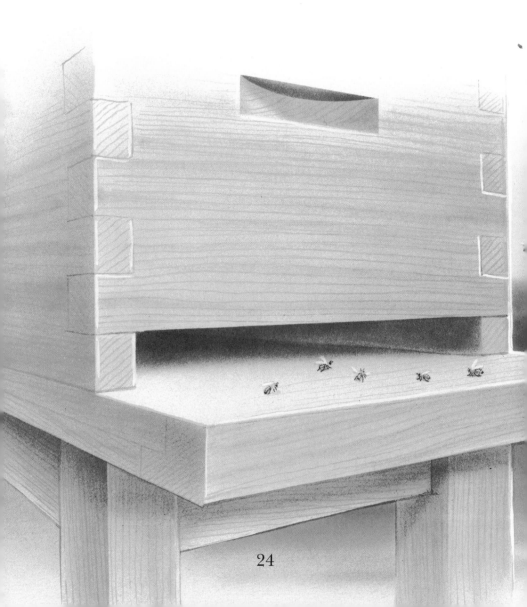

Pollen is a yellow powder.
Do you like to smell flowers?
Sometimes you end up
with pollen on your nose!

How does the bee carry pollen
back to the hive?
She has little "baskets"
on her legs.
First she chews the pollen.

She makes it into sticky balls.

She stuffs the pollen balls
into her baskets.

And off she flies!

All worker bees are female.

All drones are male.

They are bigger than worker bees.

They have huge eyes.

Their only job is to mate
with the queen bee.

The queen is much bigger than
drones or workers.

Worker

Drone

Queen

This queen is ready to mate.

She flies out of the hive.

All the drones fly after her.

Only one drone will mate

with the queen.

After they mate,

the drone will die.

Now the queen is ready to lay eggs—
up to 2,000 in one day.
She lays her eggs in empty cells.
When the eggs hatch,
larvae come out.
They look like tiny white worms.

Workers called nurse bees
feed the larvae.
First they feed them something
called bee milk.
After three days,
the larvae get "bee bread."
It is a mix of honey and pollen.

Soon the larvae are full-grown.
Nurse bees close the cells with wax.
The larvae change into pupae.
They grow big black eyes.
They grow skinny bee legs.

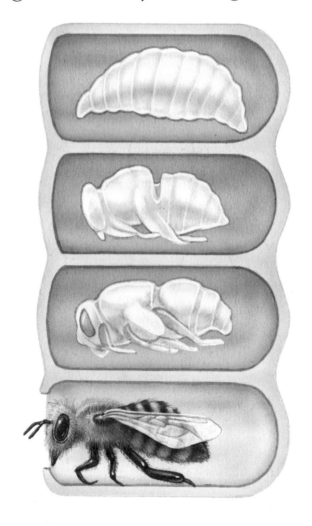

After about three weeks or so,
the young bee is ready
to chew its way out of the cell.
Right away, the worker bees
go to work.
Their first job is cleaning
the empty cells.

Older workers guard the hive.
Sometimes strange bees
try to sneak into the hive.
They want to steal honey.
Then there is a battle.

Honeybees will fight
to the death.
A worker can only sting once.
That's because its stinger gets
ripped out.
And soon the bee will die.

A hungry bear sometimes
breaks into hives.
The bees sting the soft skin
on the bear's nose.

Ouch!

The bear runs away.

He wasn't that hungry!

Beekeepers are very careful
around the hives.
They wear thick gloves.
They wear a hat
with a bee-proof net.
Some keepers use smoke.
It confuses the bees.

Then it's not as hard
to get the honey
from the hive.
Even so,
beekeepers can get stung.

Sometimes a hive has too many bees.
In late spring or early summer,
nurse bees will raise a new queen.
They move an egg to a big cell.
It is shaped like a peanut.

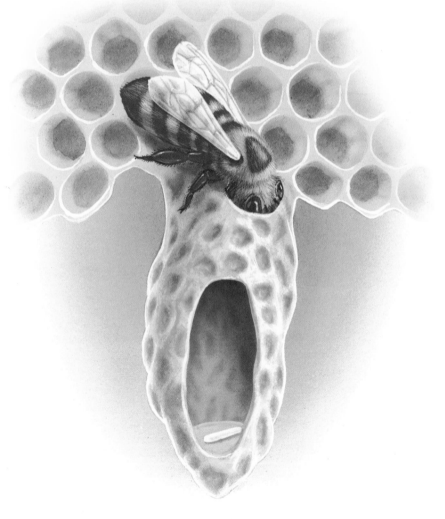

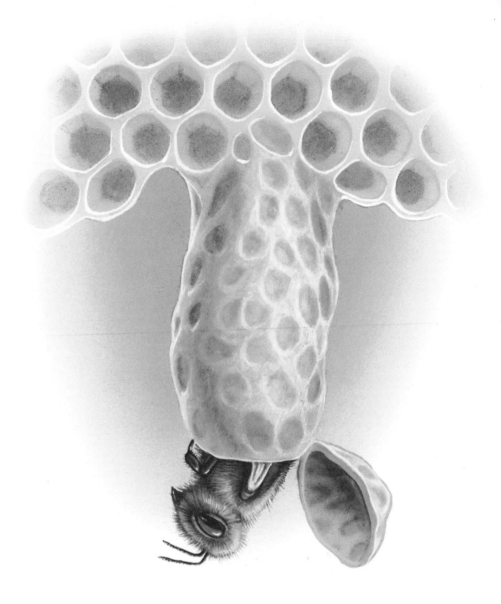

They feed the egg a special food.

It is called royal jelly.

In about 16 days

they have a new queen.

Now the old queen
must find a new home.
Thousands of bees move with her.
All at once,
they fly out of the hive.

The bees stop to rest
on a branch of an apple tree.
They form a big ball.
The queen is in the middle.
This ball of bees is called a swarm.
It can weigh five or six pounds.
That's a lot of bees!
When the beekeeper finds the bees,
he has to catch them.
That's not an easy job!

Bees do not live a long time.
A worker bee only lives
about six weeks.
Often, younger bees
throw old worker bees
out of the hive.

Before winter comes,
they kill off the drones, too.
Only a few bees will live
through the winter.

When the weather turns warm,
the queen starts to lay eggs.
Soon the hive will be full
of young bees.
It's a good thing, too.
Did you know that bees
help make flowers grow?

A worker bee
will bring pollen from one flower
to other flowers.
Strange as it seems,
this is how seeds are made!
From seeds come new flowers.

Bees may be tiny,
but they play
a big part in nature.